The MESSAGE

Sayings of Jesus

EUGENE H. PETERSON

NAVPRESS

BRINGING TRUTH TO LIFE
NavPress Publishing Group
P.O. Box 35001, Colorado Springs, Colorado 80935

The Sayings of Jesus are taken from *The Message*
by Eugene H. Peterson.

~

Other editions of *The Message* include:

The Message New Testament

The Message New Testament with
Psalms and Proverbs

The Message: Job

The Message: Psalms

The Message: Proverbs

The Message Old Testament Wisdom Books
(Job, Psalms, Proverbs, Ecclesiastes, Song of Songs)

~

ISBN 1-57683-104-3

Published in association with the literary agency of Alive
Communications, Inc., 1465 Kelly Johnson Blvd., Suite 320,
Colorado Springs, CO 80920.

Printed in the United States of America

1 2 3 4 5 6 7 8 9 10 11 12 13 14 15 / 05 04 03 02 10 00 99 98

SAYINGS OF JESUS

The arrival of Jesus signaled the beginning of a new era. God entered history in a personal way, and made it unmistakably clear that he is on our side, doing everything possible to save us. It was all presented and worked out in the life, death, and resurrection of Jesus. The message Jesus brought was, and is, hard to believe—seemingly too good to be true.

But one by one, men and women did believe it, believed the words of Jesus. That meant that everything, quite literally every thing, had to be re-centered, re-imagined, and re-thought. Jesus' words are sharp, challenging, and to the point. Ignoring them, he said, is dangerous.

Compiled from *The Message*, this collection of Jesus' words strikes us where we live today. Jesus spoke in the street language of the day, the idiom of the playground and the marketplace. Some people are taken aback by this, supposing that language from God should be stately and elevated. But one good look at Jesus—his preference for down-to-earth stories and easy association with common people—gets rid of that supposition. For Jesus is the descent of God to our lives—just as they are. His words are meant to be listened to, taken to heart, and, ultimately, to change the way we live.

"These words I speak to you are not incidental additions to your life, homeowner improvements to your standard of living. They are foundational words, words to build a life on. If you work these words into your life, you are like a smart carpenter who built his house on solid rock. Rain poured down, the river flooded, a tornado hit, but nothing moved that house. It was fixed to the rock.

"But if you just use my words in Bible studies and don't work them into your life, you are like a stupid carpenter who built his house on the sandy beach. When a storm rolled in and the waves came up, it collapsed like a house of cards."—Matthew 7:24-27

CONTENTS

Actions 7

Anger 8

Appearance 9

Attitude 10

Belief 12

The Bible 16

Caring 17

Change 19

Children 20

Christianity 21

Comfort 24

Compromise 25

Contentment 26

Criticism 28

Death 29

Depression 30

Discipline 31

Doing Good 32

Faith 35

Fear 36

Following Jesus 37

Forgiveness 42

Freedom 45

Friendship 46

Getting Ahead 47

God's Family 48

Greed 49

Grief 51

Guilt 52

Happiness 53

Hard Times 55

Heaven 57

His Kingdom 58

His Power 68

His Second Coming 69

Honesty 71

Laziness 73

Leadership 74

Life 75

Loneliness 76

Love 77

Lust 80

Marriage 81

Materialism 82

Money 83

Motives 84

Obedience 85

Peace 87

Peer Pressure 88

Persecution   89

Perseverance   90

Popularity   92

Prayer   93

Pride   96

Procrastination   98

Promises   99

Relationships   100

Responsibility   102

Rest   103

Risk   104

Sacrifice   106

Seeking God   108

Self-Image   111

Selfishness   112

Sharing   113

Status   115

Stress   116

Success   118

Telling Others About Him   119

Temptation   122

Truth   123

Violence   125

Who He Is   126

Worry   128

"Trivialize even the smallest item in God's Law and you will only have trivialized yourself. But take it seriously, show the way for others, and you will find honor in the kingdom. Unless you do far better than the Pharisees in the matters of right living, you won't know the first thing about entering the kingdom."—MATTHEW 5:19-20

"A man had two sons. He went up to the first and said, 'Son, go out for the day and work in the vineyard.'

"The son answered, 'I don't want to.' Later on he thought better of it and went.

"The father gave the same command to the second son. He answered, 'Sure, glad to.' But he never went.

"Which of the two sons did what the father asked?"

They said, "The first."

Jesus said, "Yes, and I tell you that crooks and whores are going to precede you into God's kingdom. John came to you showing you the right road. You turned up your noses at him, but the crooks and whores believed him. Even when you saw their changed lives, you didn't care enough to change and believe him."—MATTHEW 21:28-32

He went on: "It's what comes out of a person that pollutes: obscenities, lusts, thefts, murders, adulteries, greed, depravity, deceptive dealings, carousing, mean looks, slander, arrogance, foolishness—all these are vomit from the heart. *There* is the source of your pollution."—MARK 7:20-23

ANGER

"You're familiar with the command to the ancients, 'Do not murder.' I'm telling you that anyone who is so much as angry with a brother or sister is guilty of murder. Carelessly call a brother 'idiot!' and you just might find yourself hauled into court. Thoughtlessly yell 'stupid!' at a sister and you are on the brink of hellfire. The simple moral fact is that words kill." — MATTHEW 5:21-22

APPEARANCE

"Has anyone by fussing in front of the mirror ever gotten taller by so much as an inch? All this time and money wasted on fashion—do you think it makes that much difference? Instead of looking at the fashions, walk out into the fields and look at the wildflowers. They never primp or shop, but have you ever seen color and design quite like it? The ten best-dressed men and women in the country look shabby alongside them."—MATTHEW 6:27-29

So Jesus spoke to them: "You are masters at making yourselves look good in front of others, but God knows what's behind the appearance."—LUKE 16:15

"You're blessed when you're at the end of your rope. With less of you there is more of God and his rule.

"You're blessed when you feel you've lost what is most dear to you. Only then can you be embraced by the One most dear to you.

"You're blessed when you're content with just who you are—no more, no less. That's the moment you find yourselves proud owners of everything that can't be bought.

"You're blessed when you've worked up a good appetite for God. He's food and drink in the best meal you'll ever eat.

"You're blessed when you care. At the moment of being 'care-full,' you find yourselves cared for.

"You're blessed when you get your inside world— your mind and heart—put right. Then you can see God in the outside world.

"You're blessed when you can show people how to cooperate instead of compete or fight. That's when you discover who you really are, and your place in God's family.

"You're blessed when your commitment to God provokes persecution. The persecution drives you even deeper into God's kingdom.

"Not only that—count yourselves blessed every time people put you down or throw you out or speak lies about you to discredit me. What it means is that the truth is too close for comfort and they are uncomfortable. You can be

glad when that happens — give a cheer, even! — for though they don't like it, I do! And all heaven applauds. And know that you are in good company. My prophets and witnesses have always gotten into this kind of trouble."
— MATTHEW 5:3-12

"Don't be flip with the sacred. Banter and silliness give no honor to God. Don't reduce holy mysteries to slogans. In trying to be relevant, you're only being cute and inviting sacrilege." — MATTHEW 7:6

"'These people make a big show of saying the right thing,
        but their heart isn't in it.
They act like they're worshiping me,
        but they don't mean it.
They just use me as a cover
        for teaching whatever suits their fancy.'"
— MATTHEW 15:8-9

BELIEF

"Your eyes are windows into your body. If you open your eyes wide in wonder and belief, your body fills up with light."—MATTHEW 6:22

As Jesus entered the village of Capernaum, a Roman captain came up in a panic and said, "Master, my servant is sick. He can't walk. He's in terrible pain."

Jesus said, "I'll come and heal him."

"Oh, no," said the captain. "I don't want to put you to all that trouble. Just give the order and my servant will be fine. I'm a man who takes orders and gives orders. I tell one soldier, 'Go,' and he goes; to another, 'Come,' and he comes; to my slave, 'Do this,' and he does it."

Taken aback, Jesus said, "I've yet to come across this kind of simple trust in Israel, the very people who are supposed to know all about God and how he works. This man is the vanguard of many outsiders who will soon be coming from all directions—streaming in from the east, pouring in from the west, sitting down at God's kingdom banquet alongside Abraham, Isaac, and Jacob. Then those who grew up 'in the faith' but had no faith will find themselves out in the cold, outsiders to grace and wondering what happened."

Then Jesus turned to the captain and said, "Go. What you believed could happen has happened." At that moment his servant became well.—MATTHEW 8:5-13

Jesus said, "If? There are no 'ifs' among believers.
Anything can happen." —MARK 9:23

"You're not listening. Let me say it again. Unless a person
submits to this original creation—the 'wind hovering over
the water' creation, the invisible moving the visible, a baptism into a new life—it's not possible to enter God's kingdom. When you look at a baby, it's just that: a body you
can look at and touch. But the person who takes shape
within is formed by something you can't see and touch—
the Spirit—and becomes a living spirit.

"So don't be so surprised when I tell you that you
have to be 'born from above'—out of this world, so to
speak. You know well enough how the wind blows this
way and that. You hear it rustling through the trees, but
you have no idea where it comes from or where it's
headed next. That's the way it is with everyone 'born from
above' by the wind of God, the Spirit of God."
—JOHN 3:5-8

"This is how much God loved the world: He gave his Son,
his one and only Son. And this is why: so that no one need
be destroyed; by believing in him, anyone can have a
whole and lasting life." —JOHN 3:16

"It's urgent that you listen carefully to this: Anyone here
who believes what I am saying right now and aligns himself with the Father, who has in fact put me in charge, has
at this very moment the real, lasting life and is no longer

condemned to be an outsider. This person has taken a giant step from the world of the dead to the world of the living." — JOHN 5:24

"This is what my Father wants: that anyone who sees the Son and trusts who he is and what he does and then aligns with him will enter *real* life, *eternal* life. My part is to put them on their feet alive and whole at the completion of time." — JOHN 6:40

"I'm telling you the most solemn and sober truth now: Whoever believes in me has real life, eternal life."
— JOHN 6:47

"Don't be nitpickers; use your head — and heart!—to discern what is right, to test what is authentically right."
— JOHN 7:24

"I told you that you were missing God in all this. You're at a dead end. If you won't believe I am who I say I am, you're at the dead end of sins. You're missing God in your lives." — JOHN 8:24

"You don't have to wait for the End. I am, right now, Resurrection and Life. The one who believes in me, even though he or she dies, will live. And everyone who lives believing in me does not ultimately die at all. Do you believe this?" — JOHN 11:25-26

Jesus summed it all up when he cried out, "Whoever believes in me, believes not just in me but in the One who sent me. Whoever looks at me is looking, in fact, at the One who sent me. I am Light that has come into the world so that all who believe in me won't have to stay any longer in the dark."—JOHN 12:44-46

Jesus said, "So, you believe because you've seen with your own eyes. Even better blessings are in store for those who believe without seeing."—JOHN 20:29

"Ask yourself what you want people to do for you, then grab the initiative and do it for *them*. Add up God's Law and Prophets and this is what you get." — MATTHEW 7:12

"Why are you so polite with me, always saying 'Yes, sir,' and 'That's right, sir,' but never doing a thing I tell you? These words I speak to you are not mere additions to your life, homeowner improvements to your standard of living. They are foundation words, words to build a life on.

"If you work the words into your life, you are like a smart carpenter who dug deep and laid the foundation of his house on bedrock. When the river burst its banks and crashed against the house, nothing could shake it; it was built to last. But if you just use my words in Bible studies and don't work them into your life, you are like a dumb carpenter who built a house but skipped the foundation. When the swollen river came crashing in, it collapsed like a house of cards. It was a total loss." — LUKE 6:46-49

Jesus commented, "Even more blessed are those who hear God's Word and guard it with their lives!" — LUKE 11:28

"You have your heads in your Bibles constantly because you think you'll find eternal life there. But you miss the forest for the trees. These Scriptures are all about *me*! And here I am, standing right before you, and you aren't willing to receive from me the life you say you want."
— JOHN 5:39-40

"You're blessed when you care. At the moment of being 'care-full,' you find yourselves cared for." — MATTHEW 5:7

"Then the King will say to those on his right, 'Enter, you who are blessed by my Father! Take what's coming to you in this kingdom. It's been ready for you since the world's foundation. And here's why:

> I was hungry and you fed me,
> I was thirsty and you gave me a drink,
> I was homeless and you gave me a room,
> I was shivering and you gave me clothes,
> I was sick and you stopped to visit,
> I was in prison and you came to me.'

"Then those 'sheep' are going to say, 'Master, what are you talking about? When did we ever see you hungry and feed you, thirsty and give you a drink? And when did we ever see you sick or in prison and come to you?' Then the King will say, 'I'm telling the solemn truth: Whenever you did one of these things to someone overlooked or ignored, that was me—you did it to me.'"
—MATTHEW 25:34 40

Jesus answered by telling a story. "There was once a man traveling from Jerusalem to Jericho. On the way he was attacked by robbers. They took his clothes, beat him up, and went off leaving him half-dead. Luckily, a priest was on his way down the same road, but when he saw him he angled across to the other side. Then a Levite religious man showed up; he also avoided the injured man.

"A Samaritan traveling the road came on him. When he saw the man's condition, his heart went out to him. He gave him first aid, disinfecting and bandaging his wounds. Then he lifted him on to his donkey, led him to an inn, and made him comfortable. In the morning he took out two silver coins and gave them to the innkeeper, saying, 'Take good care of him. If it costs any more, put it on my bill— I'll pay you on my way back.'

"What do you think? Which of the three became a neighbor to the man attacked by robbers?"

"The one who treated him kindly," the religion scholar responded.

Jesus said, "Go and do the same." —LUKE 10:30-37

CHANGE

This Isaiah-prophesied sermon came to life in Galilee the moment Jesus started preaching. He picked up where John left off: "Change your life. God's kingdom is here."
—MATTHEW 4:17

"I've come to change everything, turn everything rightside up—how I long for it to be finished!"—LUKE 12:50

CHILDREN

At about the same time, the disciples came to Jesus asking, "Who gets the highest rank in God's kingdom?"

For an answer Jesus called over a child, whom he stood in the middle of the room, and said, "I'm telling you, once and for all, that unless you return to square one and start over like children, you're not even going to get a look at the kingdom, let alone get in. Whoever becomes simple and elemental again, like this child, will rank high in God's kingdom. What's more, when you receive the child-like on my account, it's the same as receiving me." —MATTHEW 18:1-5

One day children were brought to Jesus in the hope that he would lay hands on them and pray over them. The disciples shooed them off. But Jesus intervened: "Let the children alone, don't prevent them from coming to me. God's kingdom is made up of people like these." After laying hands on them, he left.—MATTHEW 19:13-15

"Let me tell you why you are here. You're here to be salt-seasoning that brings out the God-flavors of this earth. If you lose your saltiness, how will people taste godliness? You've lost your usefulness and will end up in the garbage.

"Here's another way to put it: You're here to be light, bringing out the God-colors in the world. God is not a secret to be kept. We're going public with this, as public as a city on a hill. If I make you light-bearers, you don't think I'm going to hide you under a bucket, do you? I'm putting you on a light stand. Now that I've put you there on a hilltop, on a light stand—shine! Keep open house; be generous with your lives. By opening up to others, you'll prompt people to open up with God, this generous Father in heaven."—MATTHEW 5:13-16

"In a word, what I'm saying is, *Grow up.* You're kingdom subjects. Now live like it. Live out your God-created identity. Live generously and graciously toward others, the way God lives toward you."—MATTHEW 5:48

"Bring health to the sick. . . . Touch the untouchables. . . . You have been treated generously, so live generously."
—MATTHEW 10:8

But Jesus was matter-of-fact: "Yes—and if you embrace this kingdom life and don't doubt God, you'll not only do

minor feats like I did to the fig tree, but also triumph over huge obstacles. This mountain, for instance, you'll tell, 'Go jump in the lake,' and it will jump. Absolutely everything, ranging from small to large, as you make it a part of your believing prayer, gets included as you lay hold of God."
—MATTHEW 21:21-22

Then he said, "Go into the world. Go everywhere and announce the Message of God's good news to one and all. Whoever believes and is baptized is saved; whoever refuses to believe is damned."—MARK 16:15

"This is war, and there is no neutral ground. If you're not on my side, you're the enemy; if you're not helping, you're making things worse."—LUKE 11:23

"But the time is coming—it has, in fact, come—when what you're called will not matter and where you go to worship will not matter.

"It's who you are and the way you live that count before God. Your worship must engage your spirit in the pursuit of truth. That's the kind of people the Father is out looking for: those who are simply and honestly *themselves* before him in their worship. God is sheer being itself—Spirit. Those who worship him must do it out of their very being, their spirits, their true selves, in adoration."
—JOHN 4:23-24

Jesus once again addressed them: "I am the world's Light. No one who follows me stumbles around in the darkness. I provide plenty of light to live in." —JOHN 8:12

"If any of you wants to serve me, then follow me. Then you'll be where I am, ready to serve at a moment's notice. The Father will honor and reward anyone who serves me." —JOHN 12:26

"I am the Vine, you are the branches. When you're joined with me and I with you, the relation intimate and organic, the harvest is sure to be abundant. Separated, you can't produce a thing." —JOHN 15:5

COMFORT

"Are you tired? Worn out? Burned out on religion? Come to me. Get away with me and you'll recover your life. I'll show you how to take a real rest." —MATTHEW 11:28

"I've told you all this so that trusting me, you will be unshakable and assured, deeply at peace. In this godless world you will continue to experience difficulties. But take heart! I've conquered the world." —JOHN 16:33

"Courage! It's me. Don't be afraid." —MARK 6:50

COMPROMISE

"Stand up for me against world opinion and I'll stand up for you before my Father in heaven. If you turn tail and run, do you think I'll cover for you?"—MATTHEW 10:32-33

"I know you inside and out, and find little to my liking. You're not cold, you're not hot—far better to be either cold or hot! You're stale. You're stagnant. You make me want to vomit."
—REVELATION 3:15-16

"You're blessed when you're content with just who you are—no more, no less. That's the moment you find yourselves proud owners of everything that can't be bought."
—MATTHEW 5:5

"If you decide for God, living a life of God-worship, it follows that you don't fuss about what's on the table at mealtimes or whether the clothes in your closet are in fashion. There is far more to your life than the food you put in your stomach, more to your outer appearance than the clothes you hang on your body. Look at the birds, free and unfettered, not tied down to a job description, careless in the care of God. And you count far more to him than birds."
—MATTHEW 6:25-26

"If God gives such attention to the appearance of wildflowers—most of which are never even seen—don't you think he'll attend to you, take pride in you, do his best for you? What I'm trying to do here is to get you to relax, to not be so preoccupied with *getting*, so you can respond to God's *giving*. People who don't know God and the way he works fuss over these things, but you know both God and how he works. Steep your life in God-reality, God-initiative, God-provisions. Don't worry about missing out. You'll find all your everyday human concerns will be met.

"Give your entire attention to what God is doing right now, and don't get worked up about what may or may not

happen tomorrow. God will help you deal with whatever
hard things come up when the time comes."
—MATTHEW 6:30-34

"What I'm saying is, If you walk around with your nose in
the air, you're going to end up flat on your face. But if
you're content to be simply yourself, you will become
more than yourself."—LUKE 14:11

CRITICISM

"Don't pick on people, jump on their failures, criticize their faults — unless, of course, you want the same treatment. That critical spirit has a way of boomeranging. It's easy to see a smudge on your neighbor's face and be oblivious to the ugly sneer on your own. Do you have the nerve to say, 'Let me wash your face for you,' when your own face is distorted by contempt? It's this whole traveling road-show mentality all over again, playing a holier-than-thou part instead of just living your part. Wipe that ugly sneer off your own face, and you might be fit to offer a washcloth to your neighbor." — MATTHEW 7:1-5

"Let me tell you something: Every one of these careless words is going to come back to haunt you. There will be a time of Reckoning. Words are powerful; take them seriously. Words can be your salvation. Words can also be your damnation." — MATTHEW 12:36-37

"Count yourself blessed every time someone cuts you down or throws you out, every time someone smears or blackens your name to discredit me. What it means is that the truth is too close for comfort and that that person is uncomfortable." — LUKE 6:22

"Be easy on people; you'll find life a lot easier."
— LUKE 6:37

DEATH

"First things first. Your business is life, not death. Follow
me. Pursue life." —MATTHEW 8:22

"I say this with absolute confidence. If you practice what
I'm telling you, you'll never have to look death in the
face." —JOHN 8:51

"Don't let this throw you. You trust God, don't you? Trust
me. There is plenty of room for you in my Father's home.
If that weren't so, would I have told you that I'm on my
way to get a room ready for you? And if I'm on my way to
get your room ready, I'll come back and get you so you
can live where I live. And you already know the road I'm
taking." —JOHN 14:1-4

DEPRESSION

"Are you tired? Worn out? Burned out on religion? Come to me. Get away with me and you'll recover your life. I'll show you how to take a real rest. Walk with me and work with me—watch how I do it. Learn the unforced rhythms of grace. I won't lay anything heavy or ill-fitting on you. Keep company with me and you'll learn to live freely and lightly."—MATTHEW 11:28-30

ISCIPLINE

"You're blessed when your commitment to God provokes persecution. The persecution drives you even deeper into God's kingdom." —MATTHEW 5:10

"When you practice some appetite-denying discipline to better concentrate on God, don't make a production out of it. It might turn you into a small-time celebrity but it won't make you a saint. If you 'go into training' inwardly, act normal outwardly. Shampoo and comb your hair, brush your teeth, wash your face. God doesn't require attention-getting devices. He won't overlook what you are doing; he'll reward you well." —MATTHEW 6:16-18

DOING GOOD

"Be especially careful when you are trying to be good so that you don't make a performance out of it. It might be good theater, but the God who made you won't be applauding."—Matthew 6:1

"When you do something for someone else, don't call attention to yourself. You've seen them in action, I'm sure—'playactors' I call them—treating prayer meeting and street corner alike as a stage, acting compassionate as long as someone is watching, playing to the crowds. They get applause, true, but that's all they get. When you help someone out, don't think about how it looks. Just do it—quietly and unobtrusively. That is the way your God, who conceived you in love, working behind the scenes, helps you out."—Matthew 6:2-4

"A good person produces good deeds and words season after season. An evil person is a blight on the orchard."
—Matthew 12:35

"Then those 'sheep' are going to say, 'Master, what are you talking about? When did we ever see you hungry and feed you, thirsty and give you a drink? And when did we ever see you sick or in prison and come to you?' Then the King will say, 'I'm telling the solemn truth: Whenever you did one of these things to someone overlooked or ignored, that was me—you did it to me.'"—Matthew 25:37-40

"Here is a simple rule of thumb for behavior: Ask yourself what you want people to do for you; then grab the initiative and do it for *them*! If you only love the lovable, do you expect a pat on the back? Run-of-the-mill sinners do that. If you only help those who help you, do you expect a medal? Garden-variety sinners do that. If you only give for what you hope to get out of it, do you think that's charity? The stingiest of pawnbrokers does that.

"I tell you, love your enemies. Help and give without expecting a return. You'll never—I promise—regret it. Live out this God-created identity the way our Father lives toward us, generously and graciously, even when we're at our worst. Our Father is kind; you be kind."—LUKE 6:31-36

Jesus answered by telling a story. "There was once a man traveling from Jerusalem to Jericho. On the way he was attacked by robbers. They took his clothes, beat him up, and went off leaving him half-dead. Luckily, a priest was on his way down the same road, but when he saw him he angled across to the other side. Then a Levite religious man showed up; he also avoided the injured man.

"A Samaritan traveling the road came on him. When he saw the man's condition, his heart went out to him. He gave him first aid, disinfecting and bandaging his wounds. Then he lifted him on to his donkey, led him to an inn, and made him comfortable. In the morning he took out two silver coins and gave them to the innkeeper, saying, 'Take good care of him. If it costs any more, put it on my bill—I'll pay you on my way back.'

"What do you think? Which of the three became a neighbor to the man attacked by robbers?"

"The one who treated him kindly," the religion scholar responded.

Jesus said, "Go and do the same." —LUKE 10:30-37

"The simple truth is that if you had a mere kernel of faith, a poppy seed, say, you would tell this mountain, 'Move!' and it would move. There is nothing you wouldn't be able to tackle."—MATTHEW 17:20

But Jesus was matter-of-fact: "Yes—and if you embrace this kingdom life and don't doubt God, you'll not only do minor feats like I did to the fig tree, but also triumph over huge obstacles. This mountain, for instance, you'll tell, 'Go jump in the lake,' and it will jump. Absolutely everything, ranging from small to large, as you make it a part of your believing prayer, gets included as you lay hold of God."—MATTHEW 21:21-22

But the Master said, "You don't need *more* faith. There is no 'more' or 'less' in faith. If you have a bare kernel of faith, say the size of a poppy seed, you could say to this sycamore tree, 'Go jump in the lake,' and it would do it."—LUKE 17:6

FEAR

"Don't be bluffed into silence by the threats of bullies. There's nothing they can do to your soul, your core being. Save your fear for God, who holds your entire life—body and soul—in his hands."—MATTHEW 10:28

Jesus reprimanded the disciples: "Why are you such cowards? Don't you have any faith at all?"—MARK 4:40

"Don't be naive. Some people will impugn your motives, others will smear your reputation—just because you believe in me."—MATTHEW 10:17

"If you don't go all the way with me, through thick and thin, you don't deserve me. If your first concern is to look after yourself, you'll never find yourself. But if you forget about yourself and look to me, you'll find both yourself and me."—MATTHEW 10:38-39

"This is war, and there is no neutral ground. If you're not on my side, you're the enemy; if you're not helping, you're making things worse."—MATTHEW 12:30

Then Jesus went to work on his disciples. "Anyone who intends to come with me has to let me lead. You're not in the driver's seat; *I* am. Don't run from suffering; embrace it. Follow me and I'll show you how. Self-help is no help at all. Self-sacrifice is the way, my way, to finding yourself, your true self. What kind of deal is it to get everything you want but lose yourself? What could you ever trade your soul for?"—MATTHEW 16:24-26

"If your hand or your foot gets in the way of God, chop it off and throw it away. You're better off maimed or lame and alive than the proud owners of two hands and two feet, godless in a furnace of eternal fire. And if your eye distracts

you from God, pull it out and throw it away. You're better
off one-eyed and alive than exercising your twenty-twenty
vision from inside the fire of hell."
—MATTHEW 18:8-9

Jesus replied, "Yes, you have followed me. In the re-
creation of the world, when the Son of Man will rule glori-
ously, you who have followed me will also rule, starting
with the twelve tribes of Israel. And not only you, but anyone who sacrifices home, family, fields—whatever—
because of me will get it all back a hundred times over, not
to mention the considerable bonus of eternal life. This is
the Great Reversal: many of the first ending up last, and
the last first."—MATTHEW 19:28-30

Calling the crowd to join his disciples, he said, "Anyone
who intends to come with me has to let me lead. You're
not in the driver's seat; I am. Don't run from suffering;
embrace it. Follow me and I'll show you how."
—MARK 8:34

"If any of you are embarrassed over me and the way I'm
leading you when you get around your fickle and unfocused friends, know that you'll be an even greater embarrassment to the Son of Man when he arrives in all the
splendor of God, his Father, with an army of the holy
angels."—MARK 8:38

He sat down and summoned the Twelve. "So you want first place? Then take the last place. Be the servant of all."—MARK 9:35

Jesus was matter-of-fact: "Embrace this God-life. Really embrace it, and nothing will be too much for you. This mountain, for instance: Just say, 'Go jump in the lake'—no shuffling or shilly-shallying—and it's as good as done. That's why I urge you to pray for absolutely everything, ranging from small to large. Include everything as you embrace this God-life, and you'll get God's everything."
—MARK 11:22-24

"Stand up for me among the people you meet and the Son of Man will stand up for you before all God's angels. But if you pretend you don't know me, do you think I'll defend you before God's angels?

"If you bad-mouth the Son of Man out of misunderstanding or ignorance, that can be overlooked. But if you're knowingly attacking God himself, taking aim at the Holy Spirit, that won't be overlooked."—LUKE 12:8-10

"Anyone who comes to me but refuses to let go of father, mother, spouse, children, brothers, sisters—yes, even one's own self!—can't be my disciple. Anyone who won't shoulder his own cross and follow behind me can't be my disciple.

"Is there anyone here who, planning to build a new house, doesn't first sit down and figure the cost so you'll know if you can complete it? If you only get the foundation laid and then run out of money, you're going to look pretty foolish. Everyone passing by will poke fun at you: 'He started something he couldn't finish.'

"Or can you imagine a king going into battle against another king without first deciding whether it is possible with his ten thousand troops to face the twenty thousand troops of the other? And if he decides he can't, won't he send an emissary and work out a truce?

"Simply put, if you're not willing to take what is dearest to you, whether plans or people, and kiss it goodbye, you can't be my disciple."—LUKE 14:26-33

"But the time is coming—it has, in fact, come—when what you're called will not matter and where you go to worship will not matter.

"It's who you are and the way you live that count before God. Your worship must engage your spirit in the pursuit of truth. That's the kind of people the Father is out looking for: those who are simply and honestly *themselves* before him in their worship. God is sheer being itself— Spirit. Those who worship him must do it out of their very being, their spirits, their true selves, in adoration."
—JOHN 4:23-24

Jesus once again addressed them: "I am the world's Light. No one who follows me stumbles around in the darkness. I provide plenty of light to live in."—JOHN 8:12

"If any of you wants to serve me, then follow me. Then you'll be where I am, ready to serve at a moment's notice. The Father will honor and reward anyone who serves me."—JOHN 12:26

Jesus said, "I am the Road, also the Truth, also the Life. No one gets to the Father apart from me."—JOHN 14:6

"In prayer there is a connection between what God does and what you do. You can't get forgiveness from God, for instance, without also forgiving others. If you refuse to do your part, you cut yourself off from God's part."
—MATTHEW 6:14-15

"There's nothing done or said that can't be forgiven. But if you deliberately persist in your slanders against God's Spirit, you are repudiating the very One who forgives. If you reject the Son of Man out of some misunderstanding, the Holy Spirit can forgive you, but when you reject the Holy Spirit, you're sawing off the branch on which you're sitting, severing by your own perversity all connection with the One who forgives."—MATTHEW 12:31-32

At that point Peter got up the nerve to ask, "Master, how many times do I forgive a brother or sister who hurts me? Seven?"

Jesus replied, "Seven! Hardly. Try seventy times seven.

"The kingdom of God is like a king who decided to square accounts with his servants. As he got under way, one servant was brought before him who had run up a debt of a hundred thousand dollars. He couldn't pay up, so the king ordered the man, along with his wife, children, and goods, to be auctioned off at the slave market.

"The poor wretch threw himself at the king's feet and

begged, 'Give me a chance and I'll pay it all back.'
Touched by his plea, the king let him off, erasing the debt.

"The servant was no sooner out of the room when he
came upon one of his fellow servants who owed him ten
dollars. He seized him by the throat and demanded, 'Pay
up. Now!'

"The poor wretch threw himself down and begged,
'Give me a chance and I'll pay it all back.' But he wouldn't
do it. He had him arrested and put in jail until the debt was
paid. When the other servants saw this going on, they were
outraged and brought a detailed report to the king.

"The king summoned the man and said, 'You evil servant! I forgave your entire debt when you begged me for
mercy. Shouldn't you be compelled to be merciful to your
fellow servant who asked for mercy?' The king was furious
and put the screws to the man until he paid back his entire
debt. And that's exactly what my Father in heaven is going
to do to each one of you who doesn't forgive unconditionally anyone who asks for mercy."—MATTHEW 18:21-35

"Listen to this carefully. I'm warning you. There's nothing
done or said that can't be forgiven. But if you persist in
your slanders against God's Holy Spirit, you are repudiating the very One who forgives, sawing off the branch on
which you're sitting, severing by your own perversity all
connection with the One who forgives."—MARK 3:28-29

"And when you assume the posture of prayer, remember
that it's not all asking. If you have anything against

someone, forgive—only then will your heavenly Father be inclined to also wipe your slate clean of sins."—MARK 11:25

Jesus said to him, "Simon, I have something to tell you."

"Oh? Tell me."

"Two men were in debt to a banker. One owed five hundred silver pieces, the other fifty. Neither of them could pay up, and so the banker canceled both debts. Which of the two would be more grateful?"

Simon answered, "I suppose the one who was forgiven the most."

"That's right," said Jesus. Then turning to the woman, but speaking to Simon, he said, "Do you see this woman? I came to your home; you provided no water for my feet, but she rained tears on my feet and dried them with her hair. You gave me no greeting, but from the time I arrived she hasn't quit kissing my feet. You provided nothing for freshening up, but she has soothed my feet with perfume. ·Impressive, isn't it? She was forgiven many, many sins, and so she is very, very grateful. If the forgiveness is minimal, the gratitude is minimal."

Then he spoke to her: "I forgive your sins."

—LUKE 7:40-48

"If you forgive someone's sins, they're gone for good. If you don't forgive sins, what are you going to do with them?"—JOHN 20:23

FREEDOM

"Look at the birds, free and unfettered, not tied down to a
job description, careless in the care of God. And you count
far more to him than birds."—MATTHEW 6:26

Then Jesus turned to the Jews who had claimed to believe
in him. "If you stick with this, living out what I tell you,
you are my disciples for sure. Then you will experience
for yourselves the truth, and the truth will free you."
—JOHN 8:31-32

"So if the Son sets you free, you are free through and
through."—JOHN 8:36

"If a fellow believer hurts you, go and tell him—work it out between the two of you. If he listens, you've made a friend."—MATTHEW 18:15

"If any of you are embarrassed over me and the way I'm leading you when you get around your fickle and unfocused friends, know that you'll be an even greater embarrassment to the Son of Man when he arrives in all the splendor of God, his Father, with an army of the holy angels."—MARK 8:38

"Stand up for me among the people you meet and the Son of Man will stand up for you before all God's angels. But if you pretend you don't know me, do you think I'll defend you before God's angels?"

"If you bad-mouth the Son of Man out of misunderstanding or ignorance, that can be overlooked. But if you're knowingly attacking God himself, taking aim at the Holy Spirit, that won't be overlooked."—LUKE 12:8-10

"This is the very best way to love. Put your life on the line for your friends."—JOHN 15:13

"Listen carefully to what I am saying—and be wary of the shrewd advice that tells you how to get ahead in the world on your own. Giving, not getting, is the way. Generosity begets generosity. Stinginess impoverishes."
—MARK 4:24-25

"Give away your life; you'll find life given back, but not merely given back—given back with bonus and blessing. Giving, not getting, is the way. Generosity begets generosity."—LUKE 6:38

GOD'S FAMILY

"You're blessed when you can show people how to cooperate instead of compete or fight. That's when you discover who you really are, and your place in God's family."—MATTHEW 5:9

"Obedience is thicker than blood. The person who obeys God's will is my brother and sister and mother."
—MARK 3:35

"Don't hoard treasure down here where it gets eaten by moths and corroded by rust or—worse!—stolen by burglars. Stockpile treasure in heaven, where it's safe from moth and rust and burglars. It's obvious, isn't it? The place where your treasure is, is the place you will most want to be, and end up being."—MATTHEW 6:19-21

"Give away your life; you'll find life given back, but not merely given back—given back with bonus and blessing. Giving, not getting, is the way. Generosity begets generosity."—LUKE 6:38

"Your eye is a lamp, lighting up your whole body. If you live wide-eyed in wonder and belief, your body fills up with light. If you live squinty-eyed in greed and distrust, your body is a dank cellar."—LUKE 11:34

Speaking to the people, he went on, "Take care! Protect yourself against the least bit of greed. Life is not defined by what you have, even when you have a lot."

Then he told them this story: "The farm of a certain rich man produced a terrific crop. He talked to himself: 'What can I do? My barn isn't big enough for this harvest.' Then he said, 'Here's what I'll do: I'll tear down my barns and build bigger ones. Then I'll gather in all my grain and goods, and I'll say to myself, "Self, you've done well! You've got it made and can now retire. Take it easy and have the time of your life!"'

"Just then God showed up and said, 'Fool! Tonight you die. And your barnful of goods—who gets it?'

"That's what happens when you fill your barn with Self and not with God."—LUKE 12:15-21

"You're blessed when you feel you've lost what is most dear to you. Only then can you be embraced by the One most dear to you." — MATTHEW 5:4

Jesus refused. "First things first. Your business is life, not death. Follow me. Pursue life." — MATTHEW 8:22

Then he spoke:

"You're blessed when you've lost it all.
God's kingdom is there for the finding . . . .

"You're blessed when the tears flow freely.
Joy comes with the morning." — LUKE 6:20-21

"I'm leaving you well and whole. That's my parting gift to you. Peace. I don't leave you the way you're used to being left — feeling abandoned, bereft. So don't be upset. Don't be distraught." — JOHN 14:27

"I've told you all this so that trusting me, you will be unshakable and assured, deeply at peace. In this godless world you will continue to experience difficulties. But take heart! I've conquered the world." — JOHN 16:33

"This is how I want you to conduct yourself in these matters. If you enter your place of worship and, about to make an offering, you suddenly remember a grudge a friend has against you, abandon your offering, leave immediately, go to this friend and make things right. Then and only then, come back and work things out with God."
—MATTHEW 5:23-24

"Everyone who makes a practice of doing evil, addicted to denial and illusion, hates God-light and won't come near it, fearing a painful exposure."—JOHN 3:20

Jesus said, "If you were really blind, you would be blameless, but since you claim to see everything so well, you're accountable for every fault and failure."—JOHN 9:41

"You're blessed when you're at the end of your rope. With less of you there is more of God and his rule.

"You're blessed when you feel you've lost what is most dear to you. Only then can you be embraced by the One most dear to you.

"You're blessed when you're content with just who you are—no more, no less. That's the moment you find yourselves proud owners of everything that can't be bought.

"You're blessed when you've worked up a good appetite for God. He's food and drink in the best meal you'll ever eat.

"You're blessed when you care. At the moment of being 'care-full,' you find yourselves cared for.

"You're blessed when you get your inside world—your mind and heart put right. Then you can see God in the outside world.

"You're blessed when you can show people how to cooperate instead of compete or fight. That's when you discover who you really are, and your place in God's family.

"You're blessed when your commitment to God provokes persecution. The persecution drives you even deeper into God's kingdom.

"Not only that—count yourselves blessed every time people put you down or throw you out or speak lies about you to discredit me. What it means is that the truth is too close for comfort and they are uncomfortable. You can be

glad when that happens — give a cheer, even! — for though they don't like it, *I* do! And all heaven applauds. And know that you are in good company. My prophets and witnesses have always gotten into this kind of trouble."
—MATTHEW 5:3-12

"You're blessed when your commitment to God provokes persecution. The persecution drives you even deeper into God's kingdom.

"Not only that—count yourselves blessed every time people put you down or throw you out or speak lies about you to discredit me. What it means is that the truth is too close for comfort and they are uncomfortable. You can be glad when that happens—give a cheer, even!—for though they don't like it, *I* do! And all heaven applauds. And know that you are in good company. My prophets and witnesses have always gotten into this kind of trouble."
—MATTHEW 5:10-12

"A student doesn't get a better desk than her teacher. A laborer doesn't make more money than his boss. Be content—pleased, even—when you, my students, my harvest hands, get the same treatment I get. If they call me, the Master, 'Dungface,' what can the workers expect?"
—MATTHEW 10:24-25

"Stand up for me against world opinion and I'll stand up for you before my Father in heaven. If you turn tail and run, do you think I'll cover for you?"—MATTHEW 10:32-33

"Everyone's going through a refining fire sooner or later, but you'll be well-preserved, protected from the *eternal* flames. Be preservatives yourselves. Preserve the peace."
—MARK 9:49-50

"There's no telling who will hate you because of me.

"Stay with it—that's what is required. Stay with it to the end. You won't be sorry; you'll be saved."
—MARK 13:13

"Count yourself blessed every time someone cuts you down or throws you out, every time someone smears or blackens your name to discredit me. What it means is that the truth is too close for comfort and that that person is uncomfortable. You can be glad when that happens—skip like a lamb, if you like!—for even though they don't like it, I do . . . and all heaven applauds. And know that you are in good company; my preachers and witnesses have always been treated like this."—LUKE 6:22-23

"I'm leaving you well and whole. That's my parting gift to you. Peace. I don't leave you the way you're used to being left—feeling abandoned, bereft. So don't be upset. Don't be distraught."—JOHN 14:27

HEAVEN

"Don't let this throw you. You trust God, don't you? Trust me. There is plenty of room for you in my Father's home. If that weren't so, would I have told you that I'm on my way to get a room ready for you? And if I'm on my way to get your room ready, I'll come back and get you so you can live where I live. And you already know the road I'm taking." —JOHN 14:1-4

He told another story. "God's kingdom is like a farmer who planted good seed in his field. That night, while his hired men were asleep, his enemy sowed thistles all through the wheat and slipped away before dawn. When the first green shoots appeared and the grain began to form, the thistles showed up, too.

"The farmhands came to the farmer and said, 'Master, that was clean seed you planted, wasn't it? Where did these thistles come from?'

"He answered, 'Some enemy did this.'

"The farmhands asked, 'Should we weed out the thistles?'

"He said, 'No, if you weed the thistles, you'll pull up the wheat, too. Let them grow together until harvest time. Then I'll instruct the harvesters to pull up the thistles and tie them in bundles for the fire, then gather the wheat and put it in the barn. . . . ' "

Jesus dismissed the congregation and went into the house. His disciples came in and said, "Explain to us that story of the thistles in the field."

So he explained. "The farmer who sows the pure seed is the Son of Man. The field is the world, the pure seeds are subjects of the kingdom, the thistles are subjects of the Devil, and the enemy who sows them is the Devil. The harvest is the end of the age, the curtain of history. The harvest hands are angels.

"The picture of thistles pulled up and burned is a

scene from the final act. The Son of Man will send his angels, weed out the thistles from his kingdom, pitch them in the trash, and be done with them. They are going to complain to high heaven, but nobody is going to listen. At the same time, ripe, holy lives will mature and adorn the kingdom of their Father.

"Are you listening to this?

"Really listening?"—MATTHEW 13:24-30, 36-43

Another story. "God's kingdom is like a pine nut that a farmer plants. It is quite small as seeds go, but in the course of years it grows into a huge pine tree, and eagles build nests in it.—MATTHEW 13:31-32

Another story. "God's kingdom is like yeast that a woman works into the dough for dozens of loaves of barley bread—and waits while the dough rises."—MATTHEW 13:33

"God's kingdom is like a treasure hidden in a field for years and then accidentally found by a trespasser. The finder is ecstatic—what a find!—and proceeds to sell everything he owns to raise money and buy that field." —MATTHEW 13:44

"Or, God's kingdom is like a jewel merchant on the hunt for excellent pearls. Finding one that is flawless, he immediately sells everything and buys it."—MATTHEW 13:45-46

"Or, God's kingdom is like a fishnet cast into the sea,

catching all kinds of fish. When it is full, it is hauled onto the beach. The good fish are picked out and put in a tub; those unfit to eat are thrown away. That's how it will be when the curtain comes down on history. The angels will come and cull the bad fish and throw them in the garbage. There will be a lot of desperate complaining, but it won't do any good."—MATTHEW 13:47-50

"I'm telling you, once and for all, that unless you return to square one and start over like children, you're not even going to get a look at the kingdom, let alone get in. Whoever becomes simple and elemental again, like this child, will rank high in God's kingdom."
—MATTHEW 18:3-4

"The kingdom of God is like a king who decided to square accounts with his servants. As he got under way, one servant was brought before him who had run up a debt of a hundred thousand dollars. He couldn't pay up, so the king ordered the man, along with his wife, children, and goods, to be auctioned off at the slave market.

"The poor wretch threw himself at the king's feet and begged, 'Give me a chance and I'll pay it all back.' Touched by his plea, the king let him off, erasing the debt.

"The servant was no sooner out of the room when he came upon one of his fellow servants who owed him ten dollars. He seized him by the throat and demanded, 'Pay up. Now!'

"The poor wretch threw himself down and begged, 'Give me a chance and I'll pay it all back.' But he wouldn't do it. He had him arrested and put in jail until the debt was paid. When the other servants saw this going on, they were outraged and brought a detailed report to the king.

"The king summoned the man and said, 'You evil servant! I forgave your entire debt when you begged me for mercy. Shouldn't you be compelled to be merciful to your fellow servant who asked for mercy?' The king was furious and put the screws to the man until he paid back his entire debt. And that's exactly what my Father in heaven is going to do to each one of you who doesn't forgive unconditionally anyone who asks for mercy."
—MATTHEW 18:23-35

But Jesus intervened: "Let the children alone, don't prevent them from coming to me. God's kingdom is made up of people like these."—MATTHEW 19:14

"God's kingdom is like an estate manager who went out early in the morning to hire workers for his vineyard. They agreed on a wage of a dollar a day, and went to work.

"Later, about nine o'clock, the manager saw some other men hanging around the town square unemployed. He told them to go to work in his vineyard and he would pay them a fair wage. They went.

"He did the same thing at noon, and again at three o'clock. At five o'clock he went back and found still others standing around. He said, 'Why are you standing around all day doing nothing?'

"They said, 'Because no one hired us.'

"He told them to go to work in his vineyard.

"When the day's work was over, the owner of the vineyard instructed his foreman, 'Call the workers in and pay them their wages. Start with the last hired and go on to the first.'

"Those hired at five o'clock came up and were each given a dollar. When those who were hired first saw that, they assumed they would get far more. But they got the same, each of them one dollar. Taking the dollar, they groused angrily to the manager, 'These last workers put in only one easy hour, and you just made them equal to us, who slaved all day under a scorching sun.'

"He replied to the one speaking for the rest, 'Friend, I haven't been unfair. We agreed on the wage of a dollar, didn't we? So take it and go. I decided to give to the one who came last the same as you. Can't I do what I want with my own money? Are you going to get stingy because I am generous?'

"Here it is again, the Great Reversal: many of the first ending up last, and the last first." —MATTHEW 20:1-16

"God's kingdom is like ten young virgins who took oil lamps and went out to greet the bridegroom. Five were silly and five were smart. The silly virgins took lamps, but no extra oil. The smart virgins took jars of oil to feed their lamps. The bridegroom didn't show up when they expected him, and they all fell asleep.

"In the middle of the night someone yelled out, 'He's here! The bridegroom's here! Go out and greet him!'

"The ten virgins got up and got their lamps ready. The silly virgins said to the smart ones, 'Our lamps are going out; lend us some of your oil.'

"They answered, 'There might not be enough to go around; go buy your own.'

"They did, but while they were out buying oil, the bridegroom arrived. When everyone who was there to greet him had gone into the wedding feast, the door was locked.

"Much later, the other virgins, the silly ones, showed up and knocked on the door, saying, 'Master, we're here. Let us in.'

"He answered, 'Do I know you? I don't think I know you.'

"So stay alert. You have no idea when he might arrive."—MATTHEW 25:1-13

"It's also like a man going off on an extended trip. He called his servants together and delegated responsibilities. To one he gave five thousand dollars, to another two thousand, to a third one thousand, depending on their abilities. Then he left. Right off, the first servant went to work and doubled his master's investment. The second did the same. But the man with the single thousand dug a hole and carefully buried his master's money.

"After a long absence, the master of those three servants came back and settled up with them. The one given five thousand dollars showed him how he had doubled his investment. His master commended him: 'Good work! You did your job well. From now on be my partner.'

"The servant with the two thousand showed how he also had doubled his master's investment. His master commended him: 'Good work! You did your job well. From now on be my partner.'

"The servant given one thousand said, 'Master, I know you have high standards and hate careless ways, that you demand the best and make no allowances for error. I was afraid I might disappoint you, so I found a good hiding place and secured your money. Here it is, safe and sound down to the last cent.'

"The master was furious. 'That's a terrible way to live! It's criminal to live cautiously like that! If you knew I was after the best, why did you do less than the least? The least you could have done would have been to invest the sum with the bankers, where at least I would have gotten a little interest.

"'Take the thousand and give it to the one who risked the most. And get rid of this "play-it-safe" who won't go out on a limb. Throw him out into utter darkness.'"
—Matthew 25:14-30

"When he finally arrives, blazing in beauty and all his angels with him, the Son of Man will take his place on his glorious throne. Then all the nations will be arranged before him and he will sort the people out, much as a shepherd sorts out sheep and goats, putting sheep to his right and goats to his left.

"Then the King will say to those on his right, 'Enter, you who are blessed by my Father! Take what's coming to you in this kingdom. It's been ready for you since the world's foundation.' "—MATTHEW 25:31-34

Jesus said, "No procrastination. No backward looks. You can't put God's kingdom off till tomorrow. Seize the day."—LUKE 9:62

"Steep yourself in God-reality, God-initiative, God-provisions. You'll find all your everyday human concerns will be met. Don't be afraid of missing out. You're my dearest friends! The Father wants to give you the very kingdom itself."—LUKE 12:31-32

Then he said, "How can I picture God's kingdom for you? What kind of story can I use? It's like a pine nut that a man plants in his front yard. It grows into a huge pine tree with thick branches, and eagles build nests in it."

He tried again. "How can I picture God's kingdom? It's like yeast that a woman works into enough dough for three loaves of bread—and waits while the dough rises."—LUKE 13:18-21

"Put your mind on your life with God. The way to life—to God!—is vigorous and requires your total attention. A lot of you are going to assume that you'll sit down to God's salvation banquet just because you've been hanging around the neighborhood all your lives. Well, one day you're going to be banging on the door, wanting to get in, but you'll find the door locked and the Master saying, 'Sorry, you're not on my guest list.'

"You'll protest, 'But we've known you all our lives!' only to be interrupted with his abrupt, 'Your kind of knowing can hardly be called knowing. You don't know the first thing about me.'

"That's when you'll find yourselves out in the cold, strangers to grace. You'll watch Abraham, Isaac, Jacob, and all the prophets march into God's kingdom. You'll watch outsiders stream in from east, west, north, and south and sit down at the table of God's kingdom. And all the time you'll be outside looking in—and wondering what happened. This is the Great Reversal: the last in line put at the head of the line, and the so-called first ending up last."—Luke 13:24-30

Jesus said, "You're absolutely right. Take it from me: Unless a person is born from above, it's not possible to see what I'm pointing to—to God's kingdom."

"How can anyone," said Nicodemus, "be born who has already been born and grown up? You can't re-enter your mother's womb and be born again. What are you saying with this 'born-from-above' talk?"

Jesus said, "You're not listening. Let me say it again. Unless a person submits to this original creation—the 'wind hovering over the water' creation, the invisible moving the visible, a baptism into a new life—it's not possible to enter God's kingdom. When you look at a baby, it's just that: a body you can look at and touch. But the person who takes shape within is formed by something you can't see and touch—the Spirit—and becomes a living spirit.

"So don't be so surprised when I tell you that you have to be 'born from above'—out of this world, so to speak. You know well enough how the wind blows this way and that. You hear it rustling through the trees, but you have no idea where it comes from or where it's headed next. That's the way it is with everyone 'born from above' by the wind of God, the Spirit of God."
—JOHN 3:3-8

"My kingdom," said Jesus, "doesn't consist of what you see around you. If it did, my followers would fight so that I wouldn't be handed over to the Jews. But I'm not that kind of king, not the world's kind of king."—JOHN 18:36

Jesus knew what they were thinking, and said, "Why this
gossipy whispering? Which do you think is simpler: to say,
'I forgive your sins,' or, 'Get up and walk'? Well, just so it's
clear that I'm the Son of Man and authorized to do either,
or both. . . ." At this he turned to the paraplegic and said,
"Get up. Take your bed and go home." — MATTHEW 9:4-6

"I've been given it all by my Father! Only the Father
knows who the Son is and only the Son knows who the
Father is. The Son can introduce the Father to anyone he
wants to."—LUKE 10:22

Jesus answered, "I told you, but you don't believe.
Everything I have done has been authorized by my Father,
actions that speak louder than words. You don't believe
because you're not my sheep. My sheep recognize my
voice. I know them, and they follow me. I give them real
and eternal life. They are protected from the Destroyer for
good. No one can steal them from out of my hand. The
Father who put them under my care is so much greater
than the Destroyer and Thief. No one could ever get them
away from him. I and the Father are one heart and
mind." — JOHN 10:25-30

"But the exact day and hour? No one knows that, not even heaven's angels, not even the Son. Only the Father. So keep a sharp lookout, for you don't know the timetable. It's like a man who takes a trip, leaving home and putting his servants in charge, each assigned a task, and commanding the gatekeeper to stand watch. So, stay at your post, watching. You have no idea when the homeowner is returning, whether evening, midnight, cockcrow, or morning. You don't want him showing up unannounced, with you asleep on the job. I say it to you, and I'm saying it to all: Stay at your post. Keep watch."—MARK 13:32-37

"Keep your shirts on; keep the lights on! Be like house servants waiting for their master to come back from his honeymoon, awake and ready to open the door when he arrives and knocks. Lucky the servants whom the master finds on watch! He'll put on an apron, sit them at the table, and serve them a meal, sharing his wedding feast with them. It doesn't matter what time of the night he arrives; they're awake   and so blessed!

"You know that if the house owner had known what night the burglar was coming, he wouldn't have stayed out late and left the place unlocked. So don't you be slovenly and careless. Just when you don't expect him, the Son of Man will show up."—LUKE 12:35-40

"But be on your guard. Don't let the sharp edge of your

expectation get dulled by parties and drinking and shopping. Otherwise, that Day is going to take you by complete surprise, spring on you suddenly like a trap, for it's going to come on everyone, everywhere, at once. So, whatever you do, don't go to sleep at the switch. Pray constantly that you will have the strength and wits to make it through everything that's coming and end up on your feet before the Son of Man."—LUKE 21:34-36

"I will not leave you orphaned. I'm coming back."
—JOHN 14:18

"And don't say anything you don't mean. This counsel is embedded deep in our traditions. You only make things worse when you lay down a smoke screen of pious talk, saying, 'I'll pray for you,' and never doing it, or saying, 'God be with you,' and not meaning it. You don't make your words true by embellishing them with religious lace. In making your speech sound more religious, it becomes less true." — MATTHEW 5:33-34

"Just say 'yes' and 'no.' When you manipulate words to get your own way, you go wrong." — MATTHEW 5:37

"Take this most seriously: A yes on earth is yes in heaven; a no on earth is no in heaven. What you say to one another is eternal. I mean this." — MATTHEW 18:18

"You're hopeless! What arrogant stupidity! You say, 'If someone makes a promise with his fingers crossed, that's nothing; but if he swears with his hand on the Bible, that's serious.' What ignorance! Does the leather on the Bible carry more weight than the skin on your hands? And what about this piece of trivia: 'If you shake hands on a promise, that's nothing; but if you raise your hand that God is your witness, that's serious'? What ridiculous hairsplitting! What difference does it make whether you shake hands or raise hands? A promise is a promise. What difference does it make if you make your promise inside or outside a

house of worship? A promise is a promise. God is present, watching and holding you to account regardless."
—Matthew 23:16-20

Jesus went on to make these comments:
"If you're honest in small things,
    you'll be honest in big things;
If you're a crook in small things,
    you'll be a crook in big things.
If you're not honest in small jobs,
    who will put you in charge of the store?"
—Luke 16:10-11

LAZINESS

When he came back to his disciples, he found them sound asleep. He said to Peter, "Can't you stick it out with me a single hour? Stay alert; be in prayer so you don't wander into temptation without even knowing you're in danger. There is a part of you that is eager, ready for anything in God. But there's another part that's as lazy as an old dog sleeping by the fire."—MATTHEW 26:40-41

"Be wary of false preachers who smile a lot, dripping with practiced sincerity. Chances are they are out to rip you off some way or other. Don't be impressed with charisma; look for character. Who preachers are is the main thing, not what they say. A genuine leader will never exploit your emotions or your pocketbook. These diseased trees with their bad apples are going to be chopped down and burned."—MATTHEW 7:15-16

So Jesus got them together to settle things down. He said, "You've observed how godless rulers throw their weight around, how quickly a little power goes to their heads. It's not going to be that way with you. Whoever wants to be great must become a servant. Whoever wants to be first among you must be your slave. That is what the Son of Man has done: He came to serve, not be served—and then to give away his life in exchange for the many who are held hostage."—MATTHEW 20:25-28

"Don't set people up as experts over your life, letting them tell you what to do. Save that authority for God; let him tell you what to do. No one else should carry the title of 'Father'; you have only one Father, and he's in heaven."
—MATTHEW 23:9

"Steep your life in God-reality, God-initiative, God-provisions. Don't worry about missing out. You'll find all your everyday human concerns will be met."
—MATTHEW 6:33

"First things first. Your business is life, not death. Follow me. Pursue life."—MATTHEW 8:22

"Give away your life; you'll find life given back, but not merely given back—given back with bonus and blessing. Giving, not getting, is the way. Generosity begets generosity."—LUKE 6:38

"Keep your life as well-lighted as your best-lighted room."—LUKE 11:36

"Take care! Protect yourself against the least bit of greed. Life is not defined by what you have, even when you have a lot."—LUKE 12:15

"Put your mind on your life with God. The way to life—to God!—is vigorous and requires your total attention."
—LUKE 13:24

"If you grasp and cling to life on your terms, you'll lose it, but if you let that life go, you'll get life on God's terms."—LUKE 17:33

LONELINESS

"I'll be with you as you do this, day after day after day, right up to the end of the age."—MATTHEW 28:20

"I will not leave you orphaned. I'm coming back."
—JOHN 14:18

"You're familiar with the old written law, 'Love your friend,' and its unwritten companion, 'Hate your enemy.' I'm challenging that. I'm telling you to love your enemies. Let them bring out the best in you, not the worst. When someone gives you a hard time, respond with the energies of prayer, for then you are working out of your true selves, your God-created selves. This is what God does. He gives his best—the sun to warm and the rain to nourish—to everyone, regardless: the good and bad, the nice and nasty. If all you do is love the lovable, do you expect a bonus? Anybody can do that. If you simply say hello to those who greet you, do you expect a medal? Any run-of-the-mill sinner does that."—MATTHEW 5:43-47

"What's the price of a pet canary? Some loose change, right? And God cares what happens to it even more than you do. He pays even greater attention to you, down to the last detail—even numbering the hairs on your head!"—MATTHEW 10:29-30

Abruptly Jesus broke into prayer: "Thank you, Father, Lord of heaven and earth. You've concealed your ways from sophisticates and know-it-alls, but spelled them out clearly to ordinary people. Yes, Father, that's the way you like to work."—MATTHEW 11:25-26

"Look at it this way. If someone has a hundred sheep and one of them wanders off, doesn't he leave the ninety-nine

and go after the one? And if he finds it, doesn't he make far more over it than over the ninety-nine who stay put? Your Father in heaven feels the same way. He doesn't want to lose even one of these simple believers."
—MATTHEW 18:12-14

Jesus said, " 'Love the Lord your God with all your passion and prayer and intelligence.' This is the most important, the first on any list. But there is a second to set alongside it: 'Love others as well as you love yourself.' These two commands are pegs; everything in God's Law and the Prophets hangs from them."—MATTHEW 22:37-40

"This is how much God loved the world: He gave his Son, his one and only Son. And this is why: so that no one need be destroyed; by believing in him, anyone can have a whole and lasting life. God didn't go to all the trouble of sending his Son merely to point an accusing finger, telling the world how bad it was. He came to help, to put the world right again. Anyone who trusts in him is acquitted; anyone who refuses to trust him has long since been under the death sentence without knowing it. And why? Because of that person's failure to believe in the one-of-a-kind Son of God when introduced to him."—JOHN 3:16-18

"In the same way, anyone who holds on to life just as it is destroys that life. But if you let it go, reckless in your love, you'll have it forever, real and eternal."—JOHN 12:25

78

"Let me give you a new command: Love one another. In the same way I loved you, you love one another. This is how everyone will recognize that you are my disciples —when they see the love you have for each other."
—JOHN 13:34-35

"I've loved you the way my Father has loved me. Make yourselves at home in my love. If you keep my commands, you'll remain intimately at home in my love. That's what I've done—kept my Father's commands and made myself at home in his love."—JOHN 15:9-10

"This is my command: Love one another the way I loved you. This is the very best way to love. Put your life on the line for your friends."—JOHN 15:12-13

"If you lived on the world's terms, the world would love you as one of its own. But since I picked you to live on God's terms and no longer on the world's terms, the world is going to hate you."—JOHN 15:19

"You know the next commandment pretty well, too: 'Don't go to bed with another's spouse.' But don't think you've preserved your virtue simply by staying out of bed. Your *heart* can be corrupted by lust even quicker than your *body*. Those leering looks you think nobody notices — they also corrupt." — MATTHEW 5:27-28

"If your hand or your foot gets in the way of God, chop it off and throw it away. You're better off maimed or lame and alive than the proud owners of two hands and two feet, godless in a furnace of eternal fire. And if your eye distracts you from God, pull it out and throw it away. You're better off one-eyed and alive than exercising your twenty-twenty vision from inside the fire of hell." — MATTHEW 18:8-9

He answered, "Haven't you read in your Bible that the Creator originally made man and woman for each other, male and female? And because of this, a man leaves father and mother and is firmly bonded to his wife, becoming one flesh—no longer two bodies but one. Because God created this organic union of the two sexes, no one should desecrate his art by cutting them apart."—MATTHEW 19:4-6

But Jesus said, "Not everyone is mature enough to live a married life. It requires a certain aptitude and grace. Marriage isn't for everyone. Some, from birth seemingly, never give marriage a thought. Others never get asked—or accepted. And some decide not to get married for kingdom reasons. But if you're capable of growing into the largeness of marriage, do it."—MATTHEW 19:11-12

"Don't hoard treasure down here where it gets eaten by moths and corroded by rust or—worse!—stolen by burglars. Stockpile treasure in heaven, where it's safe from moth and rust and burglars. It's obvious, isn't it? The place where your treasure is, is the place you will most want to be, and end up being."—MATTHEW 6:19-21

Jesus looked him hard in the eye—and loved him! He said, "There's one thing left: Go sell whatever you own and give it to the poor. All your wealth will then be heavenly wealth. And come follow me."

The man's face clouded over. This was the last thing he expected to hear, and he walked off with a heavy heart. He was holding on tight to a lot of things, and not about to let go.

Looking at his disciples, Jesus said, "Do you have any idea how difficult it is for people who 'have it all' to enter God's kingdom?"—MARK 10:21-23

Speaking to the people, he went on, "Take care! Protect yourself against the least bit of greed. Life is not defined by what you have, even when you have a lot."—LUKE 12:15

"What I'm trying to do here is get you to relax, not be so preoccupied with getting so you can respond to God's giving."—LUKE 12:29

M ONEY

"You can't worship two gods at once. Loving one god, you'll end up hating the other. Adoration of one feeds contempt for the other. You can't worship God and Money both."—MATTHEW 6:24

As he watched him go, Jesus told his disciples, "Do you have any idea how difficult it is for the rich to enter God's kingdom? Let me tell you, it's easier to gallop a camel through a needle's eye than for the rich to enter God's kingdom."—MATTHEW 19:23-24

Sitting across from the offering box, he was observing how the crowd tossed money in for the collection. Many of the rich were making large contributions. One poor widow came up and put in two small coins—a measly two cents. Jesus called his disciples over and said, "The truth is that this poor widow gave more to the collection than all the others put together. All the others gave what they'll never miss; she gave extravagantly what she couldn't afford—she gave her all."   MARK 12:41-44

"No worker can serve two bosses:
       He'll either hate the first and love the second
Or adore the first and despise the second.
       You can't serve both God and the Bank."—LUKE 16:13

"You're blessed when you get your inside world—your mind and heart—put right. Then you can see God in the outside world."—MATTHEW 5:8

"Be especially careful when you are trying to be good so that you don't make a performance out of it. It might be good theater, but the God who made you won't be applauding.

"When you do something for someone else, don't call attention to yourself. You've seen them in action, I'm sure— 'playactors' I call them—treating prayer meeting and street corner alike as a stage, acting compassionate as long as someone is watching, playing to the crowds. They get applause, true, but that's all they get. When you help someone out, don't think about how it looks. Just do it— quietly and unobtrusively. That is the way your God, who conceived you in love, working behind the scenes, helps you out."—MATTHEW 6:1-4

"If your first concern is to look after yourself, you'll never find yourself. But if you forget about yourself and look to me, you'll find both yourself and me."—MATTHEW 10:39

". . . Appearances don't impress me. I x-ray every motive and make sure you get what's coming to you."
—REVELATION 2:23

OBEDIENCE

"God's Law is more real and lasting than the stars in the sky and the ground at your feet. Long after stars burn out and earth wears out, God's Law will be alive and working.

"Trivialize even the smallest item in God's Law and you will only have trivialized yourself. But take it seriously, show the way for others, and you will find honor in the kingdom."—MATTHEW 5:18-19

"Knowing the correct password—saying 'Master, Master,' for instance—isn't going to get you anywhere with me. What is required is serious obedience—doing what my Father wills. I can see it now—at the Final Judgment thousands strutting up to me and saying, 'Master, we preached the Message, we bashed the demons, our God-sponsored projects had everyone talking.' And do you know what I am going to say? 'You missed the boat. All you did was use me to make yourselves important. You don't impress me one bit. You're out of here.'"
—MATTHEW 7:21-23

Jesus said, "Why do you question me about what's good? God is the One who is good. If you want to enter the life of God, just do what he tells you."—MATTHEW 19:17

Jesus said, "'Love the Lord your God with all your passion and prayer and intelligence.' This is the most important, the first on any list. But there is a second to set

alongside it: 'Love others as well as you love yourself.'
These two commands are pegs; everything in God's Law
and the Prophets hangs from them."—MATTHEW 22:37-40

"Obedience is thicker than blood. The person who obeys
God's will is my brother and sister and mother."
—MARK 3:35

"If you love me, show it by doing what I've told you."
—JOHN 14:15

"The person who knows my commandments and keeps
them, that's who loves me. And the person who loves me
will be loved by my Father, and I will love him and make
myself plain to him."—JOHN 14:21

"You're blessed when you can show people how to cooperate instead of compete or fight. That's when you discover who you really are, and your place in God's family.—MATTHEW 5:9

"I'm leaving you well and whole. That's my parting gift to you. Peace. I don't leave you the way you're used to being left—feeling abandoned, bereft. So don't be upset. Don't be distraught."—JOHN 14:27

"I've told you all this so that trusting me, you will be unshakable and assured, deeply at peace. In this godless world you will continue to experience difficulties. But take heart! I've conquered the world."—JOHN 16:33

PEER PRESSURE

He quoted a proverb: " 'Can a blind man guide a blind man?' Wouldn't they both end up in the ditch? An apprentice doesn't lecture the master. The point is to be careful who you follow as your teacher."—LUKE 6:39-40

"To you who are ready for the truth, I say this: Love your enemies. Let them bring out the best in you, not the worst. When someone gives you a hard time, respond with the energies of prayer for that person. If someone slaps you in the face, stand there and take it. If someone grabs your shirt, giftwrap your best coat and make a present of it. If someone takes unfair advantage of you, use the occasion to practice the servant life. No more tit-for-tat stuff. Live generously."—LUKE 6:27-30

"Fear nothing in the things you're about to suffer—but stay on guard! Fear nothing! The Devil is about to throw you in jail for a time of testing—ten days. It won't last forever.

"Don't quit, even if it costs you your life. Stay there believing. I have a Life-Crown sized and ready for you."
— REVELATION 2:10

"Staying with it—that's what God requires. Stay with it to the end. You won't be sorry, and you'll be saved."
—Matthew 24:13

When he came back to his disciples, he found them sound asleep. He said to Peter, "Can't you stick it out with me a single hour? Stay alert; be in prayer so you don't wander into temptation without even knowing you're in danger. There is a part of you that is eager, ready for anything in God. But there's another part that's as lazy as an old dog sleeping by the fire."—Matthew 26:40-41

Jesus told them a story showing that it was necessary for them to pray consistently and never quit. He said, "There was once a judge in some city who never gave God a thought and cared nothing for people. A widow in that city kept after him: 'My rights are being violated. Protect me!'

"He never gave her the time of day. But after this went on and on he said to himself, 'I care nothing what God thinks, even less what people think. But because this widow won't quit badgering me, I'd better do something and see that she gets justice—otherwise I'm going to end up beaten black-and-blue by her pounding.'"

Then the Master said, "Do you hear what that judge, corrupt as he is, is saying? So what makes you think God won't step in and work justice for his chosen people, who continue to cry out for help? Won't he stick up for them? I assure you, he will. He will not drag his feet. But how much of that kind of persistent faith will the Son of Man find on the earth when he returns?"—LUKE 18:1-8

"Fear nothing in the things you're about to suffer—but stay on guard! Fear nothing! The Devil is about to throw you in jail for a time of testing—ten days. It won't last forever.

   "Don't quit, even if it costs you your life. Stay there believing. I have a Life-Crown sized and ready for you."
—REVELATION 2:10

POPULARITY

"There's trouble ahead when you live only for the approval
of others, saying what flatters them, doing what indulges
them. Popularity contests are not truth contests—look
how many scoundrel preachers were approved by your
ancestors! Your task is to be true, not popular."—LUKE 6:26

"How do you expect to get anywhere with God when you
spend all your time jockeying for position with each other,
ranking your rivals and ignoring God?"—JOHN 5:44

"And don't say anything you don't mean. This counsel is embedded deep in our traditions. You only make things worse when you lay down a smoke screen of pious talk, saying, 'I'll pray for you,' and never doing it, or saying, 'God be with you,' and not meaning it. You don't make your words true by embellishing them with religious lace. In making your speech sound more religious, it becomes less true." — MATTHEW 5:33-34

"Here's what I want you to do: Find a quiet, secluded place so you won't be tempted to role-play before God. Just be there as simply and honestly as you can manage. The focus will shift from you to God, and you will begin to sense his grace.

"The world is full of so-called prayer warriors who are prayer-ignorant. They're full of formulas and programs and advice, peddling techniques for getting what you want from God. Don't fall for that nonsense. This is your Father you are dealing with, and he knows better than you what you need. With a God like this loving you, you can pray very simply. Like this:
'Our Father in heaven,
Reveal who you are.
Set the world right;
Do what's best —
    as above, so below.
Keep us alive with three square meals.

Keep us forgiven with you and forgiving others.
Keep us safe from ourselves and the Devil.
You're in charge!
You can do anything you want!
You're ablaze in beauty!
      Yes. Yes. Yes.'
"In prayer there is a connection between what God does
and what you do. You can't get forgiveness from God, for
instance, without also forgiving others. If you refuse to do
your part, you cut yourself off from God's part."
—MATTHEW 6:6-15

"If your child asks for bread, do you trick him with saw-
dust? If he asks for fish, do you scare him with a live snake
on his plate? As bad as you are, you wouldn't think of
such a thing. You're at least decent to your own children.
So don't you think the God who conceived you in love
will be even better?"—MATTHEW 7:9-11

"When two of you get together on anything at all on earth
and make a prayer of it, my Father in heaven goes into
action. And when two or three of you are together because
of me, you can be sure that I'll be there."
—MATTHEW 18:19-20

"Absolutely everything, ranging from small to large, as
you make it a part of your believing prayer, gets included
as you lay hold of God."—MATTHEW 21:22

"And when you assume the posture of prayer, remember that it's not all asking. If you have anything against someone, *forgive*—only then will your heavenly Father be inclined to also wipe your slate clean of sins."
—Mark 11:25

"Stay alert, be in prayer, so you don't enter the danger zone without even knowing it. Don't be naive. Part of you is eager, ready for anything in God; but another part is as lazy as an old dog sleeping by the fire."—Mark 14:38

"Don't bargain with God. Be direct. Ask for what you need. This is not a cat-and-mouse, hide-and-seek game we're in."—Luke 11:10

"But if you make yourselves at home with me and my words are at home in you, you can be sure that whatever you ask will be listened to and acted upon."—John 15:7

"Ask in my name, according to my will, and he'll most certainly give it to you. Your joy will be a river overflowing its banks!"—John 16:24

"Do you want to stand out? Then step down. Be a servant. If you puff yourself up, you'll get the wind knocked out of you. But if you're content to simply be yourself, your life will count for plenty."—MATTHEW 23:11-12

He sat down and summoned the Twelve. "So you want first place? Then take the last place. Be the servant of all."—MARK 9:35

"When someone invites you to dinner, don't take the place of honor. Somebody more important than you might have been invited by the host. Then he'll come and call out in front of everybody, 'You're in the wrong place. The place of honor belongs to this man.' Red-faced, you'll have to make your way to the very last table, the only place left.

"When you're invited to dinner, go and sit at the last place. Then when the host comes he may very well say, 'Friend, come up to the front.' That will give the dinner guests something to talk about! What I'm saying is, If you walk around with your nose in the air, you're going to end up flat on your face. But if you're content to be simply yourself, you will become more than yourself."
—LUKE 14:8-11

So Jesus spoke to them: "You are masters at making yourselves look good in front of others, but God knows what's behind the appearance."—LUKE 16:15

He told his next story to some who were complacently pleased with themselves over their moral performance and looked down their noses at the common people: "Two men went up to the Temple to pray, one a Pharisee, the other a tax man. The Pharisee posed and prayed like this: 'Oh, God, I thank you that I am not like other people—robbers, crooks, adulterers, or, heaven forbid, like this tax man. I fast twice a week and tithe on all my income.'

"Meanwhile the tax man, slumped in the shadows, his face in his hands, not daring to look up, said, 'God, give mercy. Forgive me, a sinner.'"

Jesus commented, "This tax man, not the other, went home made right with God. If you walk around with your nose in the air, you're going to end up flat on your face, but if you're content to be simply yourself, you will become more than yourself."—LUKE 18:9-14

PROCRASTINATION

Jesus said, "No procrastination. No backward looks. You can't put God's kingdom off till tomorrow. Seize the day."—LUKE 9:62

"And don't say anything you don't mean. This counsel is embedded deep in our traditions. You only make things worse when you lay down a smoke screen of pious talk, saying, 'I'll pray for you,' and never doing it, or saying, 'God be with you,' and not meaning it. You don't make your words true by embellishing them with religious lace. In making your speech sound more religious, it becomes less true. Just say 'yes' and 'no.' When you manipulate words to get your own way, you go wrong."
— MATTHEW 5:33-37

"A promise is a promise. What difference does it make if you make your promise inside or outside a house of worship? A promise is a promise. God is present, watching and holding you to account regardless." — MATTHEW 23:20

"You're blessed when you can show people how to cooperate instead of compete or fight. That's when you discover who you really are, and your place in God's family."
—MATTHEW 5:9

"You're familiar with the old written law, 'Love your friend,' and its unwritten companion, 'Hate your enemy.' I'm challenging that. I'm telling you to love your enemies. Let them bring out the best in you, not the worst. When someone gives you a hard time, respond with the energies of prayer, for then you are working out of your true selves, your God-created selves. This is what God does. He gives his best—the sun to warm and the rain to nourish—to everyone, regardless: the good and bad, the nice and nasty. If all you do is love the lovable, do you expect a bonus? Anybody can do that. If you simply say hello to those who greet you, do you expect a medal? Any run-of-the-mill sinner does that."—MATTHEW 5:43-47

"Here is a simple, rule-of-thumb guide for behavior: Ask yourself what you want people to do for you, then grab the initiative and do it for them. Add up God's Law and Prophets and this is what you get."—MATTHEW 7:12

"If a fellow believer hurts you, go and tell him—work it out between the two of you. If he listens, you've made a friend. If he won't listen, take one or two others along so that the presence of witnesses will keep things honest, and try again. If he still won't listen, tell the church. If he won't listen to the church, you'll have to start over from scratch, confront him with the need for repentance, and offer again God's forgiving love."—MATTHEW 18:15-17

"Don't pick on people, jump on their failures, criticize their faults—unless, of course, you want the same treatment. Don't condemn those who are down; that hardness can boomerang. Be easy on people; you'll find life a lot easier. Give away your life; you'll find life given back, but not merely given back—given back with bonus and blessing. Giving, not getting, is the way. Generosity begets generosity."—LUKE 6:37-38

Then he turned to the host. "The next time you put on a dinner, don't just invite your friends and family and rich neighbors, the kind of people who will return the favor. Invite some people who never get invited out, the misfits from the wrong side of the tracks. You'll be—and experience—a blessing. They won't be able to return the favor, but the favor will be returned—oh, how it will be returned!—at the resurrection of God's people."
—LUKE 14:12-14

RESPONSIBILITY

The Master said, "Let me ask you: Who is the dependable manager, full of common sense, that the master puts in charge of his staff to feed them well and on time? He is a blessed man if when the master shows up he's doing his job. But if he says to himself, 'The master is certainly taking his time,' begins maltreating the servants and maids, throws parties for his friends, and gets drunk, the master will walk in when he least expects it, give him the thrashing of his life, and put him back in the kitchen peeling potatoes.

"The servant who knows what his master wants and ignores it, or insolently does whatever he pleases, will be thoroughly thrashed. But if he does a poor job through ignorance, he'll get off with a slap on the hand. Great gifts mean great responsibilities; greater gifts, greater responsibilities!"—LUKE 12:42-48

REST

"Here's what I want you to do: Find a quiet, secluded place so you won't be tempted to role-play before God. Just be there as simply and honestly as you can manage. The focus will shift from you to God, and you will begin to sense his grace." — MATTHEW 6:6

"Are you tired? Worn out? Burned out on religion? Come to me. Get away with me and you'll recover your life. I'll show you how to take a real rest." — MATTHEW 11:28

Jesus said, "Come off by yourselves; let's take a break and get a little rest." For there was constant coming and going. They didn't even have time to eat.

So they got in the boat and went off to a remote place by themselves. — MARK 6:31-32

"There was once a man descended from a royal house who needed to make a long trip back to headquarters to get authorization for his rule and then return. But first he called ten servants together, gave them each a sum of money, and instructed them, 'Operate with this until I return.'

"But the citizens there hated him. So they sent a commission with a signed petition to oppose his rule: 'We don't want this man to rule us.'

"When he came back bringing the authorization of his rule, he called those ten servants to whom he had given the money to find out how they had done.

"The first said, 'Master, I doubled your money.'

"He said, 'Good servant! Great work! Because you've been trustworthy in this small job, I'm making you governor of ten towns.'

"The second said, 'Master, I made a fifty percent profit on your money.'

"He said, 'I'm putting you in charge of five towns.'

"The next servant said, 'Master, here's your money safe and sound. I kept it hidden in the cellar. To tell you the truth, I was a little afraid. I know you have high standards and hate sloppiness, and don't suffer fools gladly.'

"He said, 'You're right that I don't suffer fools gladly—and you've acted the fool! Why didn't you at least invest the money in securities so I would have gotten a little interest on it?'

"Then he said to those standing there, 'Take the money from him and give it to the servant who doubled my stake.'

"They said, 'But Master, he already has double . . .'

"He said, 'That's what I mean: Risk your life and get more than you ever dreamed of. Play it safe and end up holding the bag.'"—LUKE 19:12-26

S ACRIFICE

"Self-help is no help at all. Self-sacrifice is the way, my way, to saving yourself, your true self. What good would it do to get everything you want and lose you, the real you? What could you ever trade your soul for?"—MARK 8:35-37

Jesus said, "Mark my words, no one who sacrifices house, brothers, sisters, mother, father, children, land—whatever—because of me and the Message will lose out. They'll get it all back, but multiplied many times in homes, brothers, sisters, mothers, children, and land—but also in troubles. And then the bonus of eternal life! This is once again the Great Reversal: Many who are first will end up last, and the last first."—MARK 10:29-31

One poor widow came up and put in two small coins—a measly two cents. Jesus called his disciples over and said, "The truth is that this poor widow gave more to the collection than all the others put together. All the others gave what they'll never miss; she gave extravagantly what she couldn't afford—she gave her all."—MARK 12:42-44

"Anyone who comes to me but refuses to let go of father, mother, spouse, children, brothers, sisters—yes, even one's own self!—can't be my disciple. Anyone who won't shoulder his own cross and follow behind me can't be my disciple.

"Is there anyone here who, planning to build a new

house, doesn't first sit down and figure the cost so you'll know if you can complete it? If you only get the foundation laid and then run out of money, you're going to look pretty foolish. Everyone passing by will poke fun at you: 'He started something he couldn't finish.'

"Or can you imagine a king going into battle against another king without first deciding whether it is possible with his ten thousand troops to face the twenty thousand troops of the other? And if he decides he can't, won't he send an emissary and work out a truce?

"Simply put, if you're not willing to take what is dearest to you, whether plans or people, and kiss it goodbye, you can't be my disciple."—LUKE 14:26-33

"You're blessed when you've worked up a good appetite for God. He's food and drink in the best meal you'll ever eat."—MATTHEW 5:6

"Don't bargain with God. Be direct. Ask for what you need. This isn't a cat-and-mouse, hide-and-seek game we're in."—MATTHEW 7:7

"Don't look for shortcuts to God. The market is flooded with surefire, easygoing formulas for a successful life that can be practiced in your spare time. Don't fall for that stuff, even though crowds of people do. The way to life—to God!—is vigorous and requires total attention."—MATTHEW 7:13-14

"If your first concern is to look after yourself, you'll never find yourself. But if you forget about yourself and look to me, you'll find both yourself and me."—MATTHEW 10:39

"Whenever someone has a ready heart for this, the insights and understandings flow freely. But if there is no readiness, any trace of receptivity soon disappears."—MATTHEW 13:12

"Self-help is no help at all. Self-sacrifice is the way, my way, to finding yourself, your true self. What kind of deal is it to get everything you want but lose yourself? What could you ever trade your soul for?"—MATTHEW 16:25-26

"But anyone who examines this evidence will come to stake his life on this: that God himself is the truth."
—JOHN 3:33

"But the time is coming—it has, in fact, come—when what you're called will not matter and where you go to worship will not matter.

"It's who you are and the way you live that count before God. Your worship must engage your spirit in the pursuit of truth. That's the kind of people the Father is out looking for: those who are simply and honestly *themselves* before him in their worship. God is sheer being itself— Spirit. Those who worship him must do it out of their very being, their spirits, their true selves, in adoration."
—JOHN 4:23-24

"You have your heads in your Bibles constantly because you think you'll find eternal life there. But you miss the forest for the trees. These Scriptures are all about me! And here I am, standing right before you, and you aren't willing to receive from me the life you say you want."
—JOHN 5:39-40

"Don't be nitpickers; use your head—and heart!—to discern what is right, to test what is authentically right."
—JOHN 7:24

On the final and climactic day of the Feast, Jesus took his

stand. He cried out, "If anyone thirsts, let him come to me and drink. Rivers of living water will brim and spill out of the depths of anyone who believes in me this way, just as the Scripture says."—JOHN 7:37-38

Jesus then said, "I came into the world to bring everything into the clear light of day, making all the distinctions clear, so that those who have never seen will see, and those who have made a great pretense of seeing will be exposed as blind."—JOHN 9:39

Jesus said, "I am the Road, also the Truth, also the Life. No one gets to the Father apart from me."—JOHN 14:6

"In a word, what I'm saying is, *Grow up*. You're kingdom subjects. Now live like it. Live out your God-created identity. Live generously and graciously toward others, the way God lives toward you." —MATTHEW 5:48

"It's who you are, not what you say and do, that counts. Your true being brims over into true words and deeds." —LUKE 6:45

"Self-help is no help at all. Self-sacrifice is the way, my way, to finding yourself, your true self. What good would it do to get everything you want and lose you, the real you?" —LUKE 9:24-25

"What I'm saying is, If you walk around with your nose in the air, you're going to end up flat on your face. But if you're content to be simply yourself, you will become more than yourself." —LUKE 14:11

SELFISHNESS

"Self-help is no help at all. Self-sacrifice is the way, my way, to finding yourself, your true self. What kind of deal is it to get everything you want but lose yourself? What could you ever trade your soul for?" — MATTHEW 16:25-26

Speaking to the people, he went on, "Take care! Protect yourself against the least bit of greed. Life is not defined by what you have, even when you have a lot."
— LUKE 12:15

"When you do something for someone else, don't call attention to yourself. You've seen them in action, I'm sure — 'playactors' I call them — treating prayer meeting and street corner alike as a stage, acting compassionate as long as someone is watching, playing to the crowds. They get applause, true, but that's all they get. When you help someone out, don't think about how it looks. Just do it — quietly and unobtrusively. That is the way your God, who conceived you in love, working behind the scenes, helps you out." — MATTHEW 6:2-4

"Here is a simple, rule-of-thumb guide for behavior: Ask yourself what you want people to do for you, then grab the initiative and do it for them. Add up God's Law and Prophets and this is what you get." — MATTHEW 7:12

"Bring health to the sick. . . . Touch the untouchables. . . . You have been treated generously, so live generously." — MATTHEW 10:8

"If you only give for what you hope to get out of it, do you think that's charity? The stingiest of pawnbrokers does that." — LUKE 6:34

Give away your life; you'll find life given back, but not merely given back — given back with bonus and blessing. Giving, not getting, is the way. Generosity begets generosity." — LUKE 6:38

Then he turned to the host. "The next time you put on a dinner, don't just invite your friends and family and rich neighbors, the kind of people who will return the favor. Invite some people who never get invited out, the misfits from the wrong side of the tracks. You'll be—and experience—a blessing. They won't be able to return the favor, but the favor will be returned—oh, how it will be returned!—at the resurrection of God's people."
—LUKE 14:12-14

STATUS

At about the same time, the disciples came to Jesus asking, "Who gets the highest rank in God's kingdom?"

For an answer Jesus called over a child, whom he stood in the middle of the room, and said, "I'm telling you, once and for all, that unless you return to square one and start over like children, you're not even going to get a look at the kingdom, let alone get in. Whoever becomes simple and elemental again, like this child, will rank high in God's kingdom. What's more, when you receive the child-like on my account, it's the same as receiving me."

—MATTHEW 18:1-5

"You're blessed when you're at the end of your rope. With less of you there is more of God and his rule."
—MATTHEW 5:3

"If you decide for God, living a life of God-worship, it follows that you don't fuss about what's on the table at mealtimes or whether the clothes in your closet are in fashion. There is far more to your life than the food you put in your stomach, more to your outer appearance than the clothes you hang on your body."—MATTHEW 6:25

"What I'm trying to do here is to get you to relax, to not be so preoccupied with *getting*, so you can respond to God's *giving*. People who don't know God and the way he works fuss over these things, but you know both God and how he works. Steep your life in God-reality, God-initiative, God-provisions. Don't worry about missing out. You'll find all your everyday human concerns will be met.

"Give your entire attention to what God is doing right now, and don't get worked up about what may or may not happen tomorrow. God will help you deal with whatever hard things come up when the time comes."
—MATTHEW 6:31-34

"Are you tired? Worn out? Burned out on religion? Come to me. Get away with me and you'll recover your life. I'll show you how to take a real rest. Walk with me and work with me — watch how I do it. Learn the unforced rhythms of grace. I won't lay anything heavy or ill-fitting on you. Keep company with me and you'll learn to live freely and lightly." — MATTHEW 11:28-30

"Don't look for shortcuts to God. The market is flooded with surefire, easygoing formulas for a successful life that can be practiced in your spare time. Don't fall for that stuff, even though crowds of people do. The way to life—to God!—is vigorous and requires total attention."
—Matthew 7:13-14

"It's not going to be that way with you. Whoever wants to be great must become a servant."—Matthew 20:26

Jesus sent his twelve harvest hands out with this charge:

"Don't begin by traveling to some faroff place to convert unbelievers. And don't try to be dramatic by tackling some public enemy. Go to the lost, confused people right here in the neighborhood. Tell them that the kingdom is here. Bring health to the sick. Raise the dead. Touch the untouchables. Kick out the demons. You have been treated generously, so live generously.

"Don't think you have to put on a fund-raising campaign before you start. You don't need a lot of equipment. You are the equipment, and all you need to keep that going is three meals a day. Travel light.

"When you enter a town or village, don't insist on staying in a luxury inn. Get a modest place with some modest people, and be content there until you leave.

"When you knock on a door, be courteous in your greeting. If they welcome you, be gentle in your conversation. If they don't welcome you, quietly withdraw. Don't make a scene. Shrug your shoulders and be on your way. You can be sure that on Judgment Day they'll be mighty sorry—but it's no concern of yours now."
—MATTHEW 10:5-15

"And don't worry about what you'll say or how you'll say it. The right words will be there; the Spirit of your Father will supply the words.

"When people realize it is the living God you are

presenting and not some idol that makes them feel good, they are going to turn on you, even people in your own family. There is a great irony here: proclaiming so much love, experiencing so much hate! But don't quit. Don't cave in. It is all well worth it in the end. It is not success you are after in such times but survival. Be survivors! Before you've run out of options, the Son of Man will have arrived."—MATTHEW 10:19-23

"Don't be bluffed into silence by the threats of bullies. There's nothing they can do to your soul, your core being. Save your fear for God, who holds your entire life—body and soul—in his hands."—MATTHEW 10:28

"God authorized and commanded me to commission you: Go out and train everyone you meet, far and near, in this way of life, marking them by baptism in the threefold name: Father, Son, and Holy Spirit. Then instruct them in the practice of all I have commanded you. I'll be with you as you do this, day after day after day, right up to the end of the age."—MATTHEW 28:18-20

"Listen. What do you make of this? A farmer planted seed. As he scattered the seed, some of it fell on the road and birds ate it. Some fell in the gravel; it sprouted quickly but didn't put down roots, so when the sun came up it withered just as quickly. Some fell in the weeds; as it came up, it was strangled among the weeds and nothing came of it. Some fell on good earth and came up with a flourish, producing a harvest exceeding his wildest dreams. . . .

He continued, "Do you see how this story works? All my stories work this way.

"The farmer plants the Word. Some people are like the seed that falls on the hardened soil of the road. No sooner do they hear the Word than Satan snatches away what has been planted in them.

"And some are like the seed that lands in the gravel. When they first hear the Word, they respond with great enthusiasm. But there is such shallow soil of character that when the emotions wear off and some difficulty arrives, there is nothing to show for it.

"The seed cast in the weeds represents the ones who hear the kingdom news but are overwhelmed with worries about all the things they have to do and all the things they want to get. The stress strangles what they heard, and nothing comes of it.

"But the seed planted in the good earth represents those who hear the Word, embrace it, and produce a harvest beyond their wildest dreams."

Jesus went on: "Does anyone bring a lamp home and put it under a washtub or beneath the bed? Don't you put it up on a table or on the mantel? We're not keeping secrets, we're telling them; we're not hiding things, we're bringing them out into the open." —MARK 4:3-8,13-22

"The one who listens to you, listens to me. The one who rejects you, rejects me. And rejecting me is the same as rejecting God, who sent me." —LUKE 10:16

TEMPTATION

"If your hand or your foot gets in the way of God, chop it off and throw it away. You're better off maimed or lame and alive than the proud owners of two hands and two feet, godless in a furnace of eternal fire. And if your eye distracts you from God, pull it out and throw it away. You're better off one-eyed and alive than exercising your twenty-twenty vision from inside the fire of hell."
—MATTHEW 18:8-9

"Stay alert; be in prayer so you don't wander into temptation without even knowing you're in danger. There is a part of you that is eager, ready for anything in God. But there's another part that's as lazy as an old dog sleeping by the fire."—MATTHEW 26:41

"There's trouble ahead when you live only for the approval of others, saying what flatters them, doing what indulges them. Popularity contests are not truth contests—look how many scoundrel preachers were approved by your ancestors! Your task is to be true, not popular." —LUKE 6:26

"But anyone who examines this evidence will come to stake his life on this: that God himself is the truth." —JOHN 3:33

Jesus said, "I am the Road, also the Truth, also the Life. No one gets to the Father apart from me." —JOHN 14:6

"But the time is coming—it has, in fact, come—when what you're called will not matter and where you go to worship will not matter.

"It's who you are and the way you live that count before God. Your worship must engage your spirit in the pursuit of truth. That's the kind of people the Father is out looking for: those who are simply and honestly *themselves* before him in their worship."—JOHN 4:23

"Don't be nitpickers; use your head—and heart!—to discern what is right, to test what is authentically right." —JOHN 7:24

Then Jesus turned to the Jews who had claimed to believe in him. "If you stick with this, living out what I tell you, you are my disciples for sure. Then you will experience for yourselves the truth, and the truth will free you."
—JOHN 8:31-32

VIOLENCE

"Here's another old saying that deserves a second look: 'Eye for eye, tooth for tooth.' Is that going to get us anywhere? Here's what I propose: 'Don't hit back at all.' If someone strikes you, stand there and take it. If someone drags you into court and sues for the shirt off your back, giftwrap your best coat and make a present of it. And if someone takes unfair advantage of you, use the occasion to practice the servant life. No more tit-for-tat stuff. Live generously." — MATTHEW 5:38-42

Jesus said, "Put your sword back where it belongs. All who use swords are destroyed by swords."
— MATTHEW 26:52

Jesus said, "I am the Bread of Life. The person who aligns with me hungers no more and thirsts no more, ever. I have told you this explicitly because even though you have seen me in action, you don't really believe me. Every person the Father gives me eventually comes running to me. And once that person is with me, I hold on and don't let go. I came down from heaven not to follow my own whim but to accomplish the will of the One who sent me."
—JOHN 6:35-38

"I am the world's Light. No one who follows me stumbles around in the darkness. I provide plenty of light to live in."—JOHN 8:12

"For as long as I am in the world, there is plenty of light. I am the world's Light."—JOHN 9:5

"I am the Good Shepherd. I know my own sheep and my own sheep know me. In the same way, the Father knows me and I know the Father. I put the sheep before myself, sacrificing myself if necessary. You need to know that I have other sheep in addition to those in this pen. I need to gather and bring them, too. They'll also recognize my voice. Then it will be one flock, one Shepherd. This is why the Father loves me: because I freely lay down my life. And so I am free to take it up again. No one takes it from me. I lay it down of my own free will. I have the right to

lay it down; I also have the right to take it up again. I received this authority personally from my Father."
—JOHN 10:14-18

"You don't have to wait for the End. I am, right now, Resurrection and Life. The one who believes in me, even though he or she dies, will live. And everyone who lives believing in me does not ultimately die at all. Do you believe this?"—JOHN 11:25-26

Jesus said, "I am the Road, also the Truth, also the Life. No one gets to the Father apart from me. If you really knew me, you would know my Father as well. From now on, you do know him. You've even seen him!"
—JOHN 14:6-7

"I am the Vine, you are the branches. When you're joined with me and I with you, the relation intimate and organic, the harvest is sure to be abundant. Separated, you can't produce a thing. Anyone who separates from me is dead-wood, gathered up and thrown on the bonfire. But if you make yourselves at home with me and my words are at home in you, you can be sure that whatever you ask will be listened to and acted upon. This is how my Father shows who he is—when you produce grapes, when you mature as my disciples."—JOHN 15:5-8

The Master declares, "I'm A to Z. I'm The God Who Is, The God Who Was, and The God About to Arrive. I'm the Sovereign-Strong."—REVELATION 1:8

WORRY

"Don't fuss about what's on the table at mealtimes or if the clothes in your closet are in fashion. There is far more to your inner life than the food you put in your stomach, more to your outer appearance than the clothes you hang on your body. Look at the ravens, free and unfettered, not tied down to a job description, carefree in the care of God. And you count far more.

"Has anyone by fussing before the mirror ever gotten taller by so much as an inch? If fussing can't even do that, why fuss at all? Walk into the fields and look at the wild-flowers. They don't fuss with their appearance—but have you ever seen color and design quite like it? The ten best-dressed men and women in the country look shabby along-side them. If God gives such attention to the wildflowers, most of them never even seen, don't you think he'll attend to you, take pride in you, do his best for you?"
—LUKE 12:22-28

Peterson, Eugene H
Sayings of Jesus
10. Bible

HC   2013-107